First published by Parragon in 2010

Parragon
Queen Street House
4 Queen Street
Bath BA1 1HE, UK

Copyright © Parragon Books Ltd 2009
Design by Pink Creative Ltd

ISBN: 978-1-4075-8642-7

Printed in China

friendship

a special gift for
a special friend

PaRragon

Bath · New York · Singapore · Hong Kong · Cologne · Delhi · Melbourne

A circle is round
it has no end,
that's how long
I want to be your friend!

4

You just **reminded** me
of what's really **important** in life:

Friends
best friends.

Idgie Threadgoode, *Fried Green Tomatoes*

A loyal friend

laughs at your jokes

when they're not so good,

and sympathizes

with your problems

when they're not so bad.

Arnold H. Glasgow, Humorist

A brother is not always a friend, but a friend is always a brother.

Unknown

It is one of the blessings of
old friends
that you can afford to be stupid with them.

Ralph Waldo Emerson, Essayist, philosopher and poet

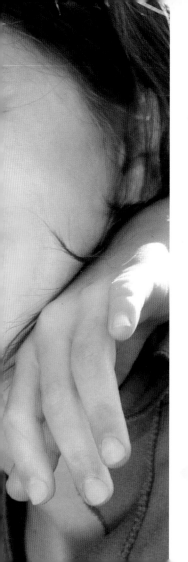

Friendship is Love

without his wings!

Lord Byron, Poet

A friend is one that knows you as you are,

understands where you have been,

accepts what you have become,
and still, gently allows you to grow.

Unknown

Few **delights** can equal the mere presence of someone we utterly **trust.**

George MacDonald, Author and poet

Hold a true friend
with both your hands.

Nigerian proverb

The best kind of friend
is the kind you can sit
on a porch and swing with,
never say a word,
and then walk away
feeling like it was the
best conversation
you've ever had.

Unknown

Count your age with friends but not with years.

Unknown

The loneliest woman in the world is a woman without a close woman friend.

George Santayana, Philosopher and essayist

Friendship
doubles
our joy
and divides
our grief.

Swedish proverb

The holy passion of friendship
is of so sweet and steady
and loyal and enduring a nature
that it will last through a whole lifetime,
if not asked to lend money.

Mark Twain, Author and humorist

We are all travellers

in the wilderness

of the world,

and the best

that we find

in our travels

is an honest friend.

Robert Louis Stevenson,
Novelist and poet

I get by with a little help

from my friends.

John Lennon, Singer, songwriter and peace activist

A best friend
is a sister that
destiny
forgot
to give you.

Unknown

The bird: a nest

The spider: a web

The human: friendship.

William Blake, Poet

If you have one
true friend
you have more than
your share.

Thomas Fuller, Churchman and historian

A friend is one of the nicest things you can have,

and one of the best things you can be.

Douglas Pagels, Author

There is nothing

worth the wear

of winning,

but laughter

and the love

of friends.

Hillaire Belloc, Writer and historian

True friendship comes when

silence between two people is comfortable.

Dave Tyson Gentry, Author

We can live without religion and meditation,
but we cannot survive without
human affection.

The Dalai Lama

A **true** friend is someone who thinks that you are a **good egg** even though he knows that you are slightly cracked.

Bernard Meltzer, Radio host

Wherever you may be it is your friends
who make your world.

Unknown

I don't remember
how we happened
to meet each other.

I don't remember
who got along with whom first.

All I can remember
is all of us together... always.

Unknown

Friends
are the
sunshine
of life.

John Hay, Statesman

I no doubt deserved

my enemies,

but I don't believe I

deserved my friends.

Walt Whitman, Poet

The miracle of friendship
can be spoken without words...
hearing unspoken needs,
recognizing secret dreams,
understanding the silent things
that only true friends know.

Unknown

60

Best friends are like diamonds,
precious and rare.

False friends are like leaves,
found everywhere.

Unknown

Friendship needs no words.

Dag Hammarskjold
Former Second Secretary-General of the United Nations

Don't walk in front of me, I may not follow,

Don't walk behind me, I may not lead,

Just walk beside me and be my friend.

Albert Carnus, Author

A friend is someone
who reaches
out for your hand...
and touches
your heart.

Unknown

I count myself in nothing else so happy as in a soul remembering my good friends.

William Shakespeare, Poet and playwright

Never shall I forget
the days I spent with you.

Continue to be my friend,

as you will always find me yours.

Ludwig van Beethoven, Composer and pianist

Some people come into our lives,
leave footprints on our hearts,
and we are never the same.

Unknown

Remember -

no man is a failure who has friends.

Clarence, Author, *It's a Wonderful Life*

There is magic in the memory of schoolboy friendships;

it softens the hearts and even affects the

nervous system of those who have no heart.

Benjamin Disraeli, Former Prime Minister

What is a friend?

A single soul dwelling in two bodies.

Aristotle, Philosopher

Friendship is born

at that moment when one person says to another:

"What! You, too? Thought I was the only one."

C S Lewis, Novelist

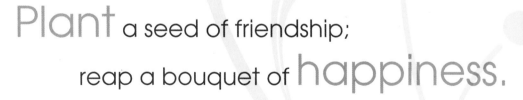

Plant a seed of friendship;

reap a bouquet of happiness.

Lois L. Kaufman, Author

I have a hand, and you have another;
put them together
and we have each other.

Girl Scout Motto

89

Promise you won't forget me, because if I thought you would, I'd never leave.

Winnie the Pooh, AA Milne

The ornament of a house is the friends who frequent it.

Ralph Waldo Emerson,
Essayist, philosopher and poet